STRANGE UNSOLVED MYSTERIES

MYSTERIES OF BIZARRE ANIMALS and FREAKS OF NATURE

Strange, Unsolved Mysteries from Tor books

Mysteries of Ships and Planes
Monsters, Strange Dreams, and UFOs
Mysteries of Bizarre Animals and Freaks of Nature
Mysteries of People and Places
Ghosts, Hauntings and Mysterious Happenings
Mysteries of Space and the Universe

STRANGE UNSOLVED MYSTERIES

MYSTERIES OF BIZARRE ANIMALS and FREAKS OF NATURE

PHYLLIS
RAYBIN EMERT
Illustrated by JAEL

A TOM DOHERTY ASSOCIATES BOOK
NEW YORK

MYSTERIES OF BIZARRE ANIMALS AND FREAKS OF NATURE

Copyright © 1994 by RGA Publishing Group, Inc.

Cover art and interior illustrations by Jael

A Tor Book
Published by Tom Doherty Associates, Inc.
175 Fifth Avenue
New York, N.Y. 10010

Tor® is a registered trademark of Tom Doherty Associates, Inc.

ISBN: 0-812-53630-4

First Tor edition: August 1994

Printed in the United States of America

0 9 8 7 6 5 4 3 2 1

For the Sanders family:
Kelly Jane, Jeremy, Amy, Dawn, and Tom

Special Thanks to
The Fairfield Free Public Library
for assistance in researching
the illustrations

Contents

Earthquake! 1

Strongheart 4

Killer Bees 8

Late, Great Dinos 12

The Snake That Took Revenge 17

Wanted: A Living Coelacanth 20

Lady Wonder 25

King 30

Bloodsuckers 33

The Killer Sea Wasp 37

Sam's Journey 42

The Archerfish 45

The "Bomber" Beetle 50

Giants of the Deep   54
Sparky   60
Man-Eating Plants   63
Electric Eel   68
Nancy   72
Sea Serpents and Lake Monsters   76
Cunning Crows   81
Buffy   84
Spiders on the Loose   87
Dolphins to the Rescue   92
Forever Friends   96
Chimp Talk   99
Strulli   103

Glossary   106
Bibliography   112

Earthquake!

It had been a beautiful, clear day in the Italian mountain villages near the town of Friuli. The only thing unusual was the behavior of the animals that evening.

Peasants working in the fields near the mountains of San Leopoldo heard unusual noises in the woods.

"Look there," said one villager as he pointed upward. "I've never seen anything like it in the region before."

The others glanced up to see more than a dozen roe deer huddled together on the slopes above the village. "There are more deer nearby with their heads down."

"That's strange," said another man.

"They're not grazing." He shrugged his shoulders. "Deer never come down into the valley this time of year."

The deer were not the only animals acting strangely. Chickens refused to enter their roosts. Cats in the village mysteriously disappeared. Mice and rats ran around freely. Cattle began bellowing, and the village dogs barked furiously. Many pets refused to enter the homes of their owners. At 9 P.M. on the evening of May 6, 1976, a powerful earthquake (6.5 on the Richter scale) thundered through the area. It destroyed or damaged nearly all structures. Numerous aftershocks turned what was left standing into rubble.

Did the animals sense the disaster that was to come? Do they possess a sixth sense that enables them to predict danger? Many people think so.

As early as 373 B.C., the Greek historian Diodorus wrote that all animals, especially rats, snakes, and even worms and beetles, left the town of Helice in masses one day. A few days later a violent earthquake struck, destroying the city, which sank into the Gulf of Corinth.

Throughout history, there have been accounts of the strange behavior of animals prior to earthquakes and other disasters. So many, in fact, that the Chinese have set up a nationwide earthquake alarm system by having their citizens carefully study animal behavior.

It paid off on February 4, 1975, when a 7.3 quake struck the city of Haicheng. The Chinese had predicted the disaster after noting the actions of panicked cattle, farm animals, and pets in the area. People had been evacuated into shelters. Animals and valuables had been removed from buildings. Although many structures were destroyed, few people died in the quake itself.

Some scientists believe that animals react to physical changes in the earth and the atmosphere just prior to an earthquake. Is there a rumbling or movement of the ground that animals detect before humans can? Do they notice changes in the magnetic and electrical fields of the earth's surface before an earthquake strikes? Or do animals possess extrasensory perception (ESP)—special powers beyond the normal five senses of touch, sight, hearing, smell, and taste?

Whether the explanation someday proves to be scientific or psychic, the reason for this unusual animal behavior is still a mystery. But one thing is certain. People who live around possible earthquake sites are paying closer attention to their pets and livestock. It could be a matter of life or death!

Strongheart

Before Rin Tin Tin, Lassie, and Benji, there was Strongheart, the first dog star in Hollywood. In the early days of motion pictures (during the 1920s), this magnificent-looking German shepherd was the top-ranked movie star and the biggest box office attraction in the world.

In a personal appearance tour across the country, Strongheart's train was met by thousands of admirers, both young and old, from coast to coast. He was awarded keys to the cities he visited, and he always stayed in the best hotel suites.

Strongheart came to America from Germany, where he was a champion police and war dog. He weighed about 120 pounds and was powerfully built. But it was his face that revealed a unique intelligence and understanding.

Allen Boone wrote about his relationship with this extraordinary dog in his book *Kinship With All Life*. Strongheart was often sent toys, which were all kept in one particular closet, by his admirers. When he felt like playing with a toy, the dog would open the closet door with his mouth, pick out one toy he liked, back out of the closet, close the door behind him, and take the toy outside.

When Strongheart was finished playing, he would bring the toy back, open the closet door, replace the toy, back out, and close the door. He did these things on his own, without a trainer guiding him, without treats, and without hand signals!

If Strongheart wanted to go outside, he opened the door himself and went out. When it was time for bed, he barked and pulled Boone into the bedroom. When it was time to get up, he barked again and tugged at Boone's pajamas. He was a superstar and used to having his own way.

One incident in particular made Boone realize how remarkable Strongheart really was. Boone was working at his typewriter on a beautiful spring morning. He began thinking about how nice it would be to stop everything and take Strongheart into the hills for a long walk.

Boone hadn't even gotten out of his chair when the back door crashed open and Strongheart ran excitedly into the room. He licked Boone's hand, rushed into the bedroom, and came out with the old sweater Boone wore whenever they went outside. After dropping the sweater at Boone's feet, Strongheart ran back to the bedroom and came back with Boone's jeans. After three more trips to the bedroom, Strongheart had brought everything they would need for their outing together.

How did Strongheart know Boone had decided they would go for a walk? There was only one way. Strongheart had read Boone's mind! In fact, he had probably been reading his mind all along, but Boone never noticed. Some people might say the dog interpreted the man's movements and gestures and concluded they were going outside. But Strongheart wasn't even in the room at the time!

Boone spent much of his time trying to establish a two-way form of telepathic communication with the animal. After a while, Boone and the dog became inseparable, and the two learned to share a special psychic connection.

There's no doubt that Strongheart was a remarkably intelligent creature who possessed powers far beyond those of the average dog. But did Strongheart have extrasensory perception? Allen Boone believed without a doubt that he did.

Killer Bees

Fifteen hundred people waited patiently on the international bridge connecting the cities of Uruguaiana, Brazil, and Passo de los Libres, Argentina. Farmers were taking their fresh fruit to market, and tourists were traveling from one country to another.

"What's taking so long?" complained one man.

"Calm down," said his companion. "It takes time for the customs agents to check everyone's papers and inspect the cargo."

"What time is it anyway? The smell of the fruit is making me hungry."

"It's ten A.M. We'll grab a bite to eat when we get off the bridge."

"What is that high-pitched noise?" a nearby woman asked. "It sounds like buzzing to me."

Before anyone could react, the air was thick with angry flying insects. A huge swarm of thousands of African bees, attracted by the fresh fruit, attacked the people on the bridge. Within seconds, the buzzing of the bees was drowned out by screams and cries of pain and terror.

The people panicked. Some ran off the bridge trying to protect their face and head from the onslaught of stings. Others jumped off the bridge into the river below.

Those who were sensitive to insect bites went into shock from the venom of multiple stings. The bees covered the fruit trucks so thoroughly they didn't look like trucks anymore.

Fire departments from both cities fought the bees for hours. When the dust had settled, it looked like a major war zone. More than one thousand people had to be hospitalized, some in serious condition. One man had been stung sixty times in the face and head.

This wasn't a scene from a television movie of the week. It really happened on December 5, 1975. The question is, how did normally gentle, productive honeybees turn into these fierce and vicious creatures?

It all began in 1957. A geneticist named Warwick Kerr was conducting bee-breeding research experiments at the University of São Paulo in Brazil. Kerr wanted to increase the honey production of the Brazilian bees, which were the gentle, European type.

Kerr decided to crossbreed African queen bees with the European variety. The African type was known for its aggressive behavior and high rate of honey production. Kerr's plan was to breed a gentle, but more productive, honeybee.

Disaster struck. Twenty-six African queens were accidentally released from their hives and quickly established new colonies in the nearby forests. They began to crossbreed with the local bees, resulting in a new strain of fierce African bees. The local bees were overwhelmed and the African bees spread throughout the country and parts of South America.

The slightest disturbance causes the African bees to release alarm pheromones that act as an attack signal to the swarm. The bees react so quickly that people or animals are unable to defend themselves and may die of massive stinging.

Killer bees have been responsible for hundreds of deaths across Central and South America. For every death, thousands more have been hospitalized. The bees continue to travel northward into Mexico and the United States.

The first confirmed attack by killer bees in the United States took place on June 5, 1991, in Brownsville, Texas. A maintenance man unknowingly ran over a hive with a power lawn mower. He was stung eighteen times but survived the attack.

Once thought to be better honey producers, the African bees are now known to be responsible for a 60 to 70 percent drop in honey production in Central and South America. U.S. farmers are worried how this might affect American honey production as well as the pollination of fruit and vegetable crops that are also dependent upon bees.

Scientists are attempting to unlock the mystery of the African honeybee. They hope to find a way to allow the European bee to take back its position of dominance. In the meantime, the killer bees are here to stay.

Late, Great Dinos

The giant ten-ton dinosaur, sensing danger, lifted its enormous head to scan the horizon. Suddenly a flash of light, one hundred times brighter than the sun, filled the sky. In an instant, the largest and most ferocious creature that ever lived was burned to a cinder.

Was this how Tyrannosaurus Rex and other prehistoric beasts suddenly became extinct 65 million years ago? Some people think so.

According to Michael Allaby and James Lovelock, authors of *The Great Extinction*, an enormous object from space, weighing more than 100 billion tons and traveling twenty times faster than a rifle bullet, which moves at about 2,800 feet per second, crashed into the north Atlantic Ocean. This collision with Earth would have caused an explosion 5 billion times stronger than either of the atomic bombs dropped on Japan in 1945!

Huge amounts of water and debris would have violently shot into the atmosphere, polluting the air and blocking the sun. Darkness, flooding, earthquakes, and tidal waves throughout the world would have been the result of such an impact.

The small percentage of creatures that lived through the catastrophe would have had to exist in a darkened environment with little remaining vegetation. Few of the large animals could have survived, but many small mammals would have lived on, eating seeds, spores, and what remained of the plant life.

It might have happened this way, but no one knows for sure. Scientists disagree as to whether the dinosaurs died out quickly, as described above, or whether the process was a gradual one lasting thousands or even millions of years.

Dr. Robert T. Bakker, author of *The Dinosaur Heresies*, believes the extinction occurred gradually. The shallow seas that

covered large land areas during the Age of the Dinosaurs began to drain away from the continents. Land bridges emerged, allowing different species to travel to other parts of the world. Each species brought with it foreign parasites and bacteria. This species exchange might have unleashed new diseases among the dinosaurs from which they never recovered.

Bakker believes a meteorite or large asteroid might have struck the Earth long ago, but it killed off only the few surviving dinosaurs. The main cause of the dinosaur's disappearance was widespread unchecked disease, similar to the bubonic plague that swept through Europe in the fourteenth century.

Other extinction theories range from changes in climate to starvation to overcrowding. According to Dr. Tony Swain, an English botanist, chemist and author of numerous books including *Plants in the Development of Modern Science*, the large plant-eating dinosaurs (herbivores) ate huge quantities of flowering plants that contained large amounts of alkaloids. Did the plant-eaters die of alkaloid poisoning? If the answer is yes, then the flesh-eaters (carnivores) died soon after, since they depended on the plant-eaters for their own existence.

As time goes on, new pieces of the puzzle surrounding the death and disappearance of the dinosaurs will be uncovered. But there are still many unanswered questions. Will the riddle ever be completely solved? Until it is, it will remain one of the great mysteries.

The Snake That Took Revenge

Do animals feel the same kind of emotions that people do? There are numerous stories of grief suffered by animals when they lose a mate, an owner, or even a friend. It follows that if they feel grief, they could feel other emotions too, such as joy, depression, satisfaction, and even revenge.

Can animals feel revenge, an emotion that requires reason, thought, and action? An interesting true story about a snake's revenge was described in a book by Alexander Key called *The Strange White Doves*.

Key's uncle lived in Florida when he was a young man. One day he was clearing some of the land around his house so he could plant a garden. While he was trying to dig up an old tree stump, it broke open, revealing a pair of small brown snakes.

Key's uncle was surprised and frightened. When he saw markings on the snakes similar to a rattler's, he reacted without thinking. He swung his pickax and tried to kill the creatures.

Had the man taken a few seconds to think, he would have realized that they were harmless king snakes that killed mice and other rodents. They were more valuable to him alive than dead. But it was too late. The pickax came down like a guillotine, killing one snake instantly. The other escaped. From that day on, it began to stalk Key's uncle to take revenge for the murder of its companion.

Although the man was sorry for killing the snake, he wasn't very upset at first, even when he noticed the surviving snake start to follow him whenever he left the house. He didn't think the creature would continue this behavior for very long, but he was wrong. The king snake turned up everywhere and began to make Key's uncle very nervous.

When he was working outside near the house, the man would turn suddenly and see the snake only a few yards away. He was sure it was watching him carefully, waiting for an opportunity to strike.

The man would sit on the porch of his house and watch the snake slither up to the windows and screen door. He knew it was searching for a way to get into the house.

This went on for weeks and weeks. According to Key: "He had destroyed its home and killed its mate, and it sought revenge with the only weapon it had that might succeed against a man."

Key's uncle was in such a state of panic that he felt he had to kill the snake to preserve his sanity. He hid weapons for this purpose all over the grounds, in case the snake surprised him. The small creature continued to outsmart the man, until one fateful day the snake slithered too close and Key's uncle grabbed a hoe and killed it.

The man was haunted by the incident throughout his life. So, in a strange way, the snake did get its revenge.

Wanted:
A Living Coelacanth

It was a routine fishing trip along the coast of southern Africa for the trawler *Nerine* on December 22, 1938. Little did Captain Hendrik Goosen and his crew know that they would soon be involved in one of the most important discoveries of the twentieth century.

The trawler dragged large nets along the bottom of the Indian Ocean, trapping many different kinds of fish that were later sold. If Goosen found anything interesting or unusual in his nets, he would notify Marjorie Courteney-Latimer, curator of the East London Natural History Museum. She collected specimens for the museum and hoped to identify new or unusual species.

By the time the *Nerine* docked at New London that morning, the day was already hot and bright. Along with the usual number of small sharks, rat tails, rays, and other assorted creatures, Goosen noticed a large fish at the bottom of the pile. It was about five feet long and dark blue in color with big blue eyes. What was really unusual was its odd-looking fins that resembled legs.

Goosen notified Courteney-Latimer, who admitted she had never seen anything like it before. She took it to the museum and examined the fish closely. It was fifty-four inches long and weighed 127 pounds. The fish's blue color had changed to gray-black, and its whole body was covered with sharp, bony scales.

Courteney-Latimer quickly sent a letter and a sketch of the fish to Professor James L. B. Smith at Rhodes University, 350 miles away. She hoped he would be able to identify what she thought was a very primitive creature. By the time Smith's reply was received, the fish had been mounted to prevent total decay and its internal organs had been thrown away.

Smith believed Courteney-Latimer had made an incredible discovery. It looked very

much like a fossil fish called a coelacanth (pronounced "SEAL-uh-canth"). However, the last fish of this type had supposedly become extinct with the dinosaurs millions of years ago!

Seven weeks after the fish had been pulled from the Indian Ocean, Professor Smith finally arrived in East London to see the mounted specimen. "That first sight hit me like a white-hot blast . . ." he said. "It was true, it really was true. It was unquestionably a coelacanth."

Why all this excitement about a fish? Here was a creature that was thought to have existed 300 million years ago and was considered extinct. This fish had been identified previously only by its fossil remains, and the discovery of a living specimen was proof that the coelacanth was alive today in the twentieth century!

Smith was sure there must be other living coelacanths, and he was determined to find them. He printed and distributed posters in South African ports offering a reward for two more specimens.

Smith had no idea that it would take fourteen years for a second coelacanth to be discovered. In December of 1952, a fisherman named Ahmed Hussein caught the fish near one of the Comores Islands off the coast of

Mozambique. Although it was slightly damaged, the fish contained many of its internal organs.

A third specimen was caught in 1953, also near the Comores Islands, now thought to be the central home of the coelacanths. At this time, the French government took control of the project since the islands were French territory. Over the years dozens of specimens were caught, studied, and even presented to museums throughout the world for exhibit.

It wasn't until 1987 that underwater film was taken of live coelacanths swimming in their own environment. The next big challenge for scientists is to capture a living fish and keep it alive for observation.

The discovery of the coelacanth is an example of cryptozoology, the study of and search for hidden and as yet unidentified living animals. The coelacanth, thought to be extinct 70 to 80 million years ago, was discovered by chance. What other mysterious creatures are waiting to be detected in the depths of the sea or other unexplored regions of the world? Time will tell.

Lady Wonder

Lady Wonder read people's minds and located lost valuables. She correctly predicted the outcome of elections and sporting events. What was especially amazing was that Lady Wonder was only a year old when she began to exhibit these special talents!

She became famous in the late 1920s for her psychic ability. For nearly thirty years Lady Wonder was the subject of many newspaper and magazine articles. She couldn't speak very well so she used a typewriter to communicate with others.

In case you haven't guessed, Lady Wonder was a horse—an incredible black-and-white filly. Owned by Mrs. Claudia Fonda of Richmond, Virginia, Lady Wonder first made headlines in 1928 with her ability to solve arithmetic problems.

Mrs. Fonda developed a special typewriter for the horse to use, with extra large keys made of soft rubber that could be easily operated. The typewriter had the alphabet and the numbers zero through nine on the keys. The horse touched her muzzle to the proper key and a number or letter would flip up. In this way, Lady Wonder could talk to anyone.

In a 1932 interview with a reporter from a Richmond newspaper, Lady was asked who would be nominated by the Democratic party for president of the United States. The horse typed "ROO," then stopped, looked around, and typed out "I can't spell the name." The Democratic presidential candidate turned out to be Franklin Roosevelt, who was elected president four straight times, in 1932, 1936, 1940, and 1944.

The reporter thought that Mrs. Fonda could have given special signals or made gestures to Lady Wonder to tell her how to respond. So the reporter then asked the horse to type out her middle name, which was not known to Mrs. Fonda. The horse responded correctly and also typed out numbers the reporter and her assistant had written on hidden pieces of paper.

Many people questioned Lady Wonder's abilities until she touched them directly. Author Morey Bernstein, who wrote about reincarnation in *The Search for Bridey Murphy*, lost his luggage on a plane trip from Denver, Colorado, to Houston, Texas. The airline couldn't locate the bags, which contained important papers and information. Bernstein consulted Lady Wonder, who said the luggage was sitting in a New York airport. Much to the embarrassment of the airline, that's exactly where it turned out to be.

When Lady Wonder regularly predicted the results of horse races, racing officials put a stop to it. She even helped the police find missing children successfully.

Over the years, this amazing horse was an object of study by doctors, professors, and psychologists. They often insisted that Lady's owner leave the testing area so the horse wouldn't be influenced in her responses by any gestures or bodily movements. Then a screen was placed between Lady and her questioners so she wouldn't respond to gestures unknowingly made by them. The horse provided answers so quickly and correctly that Dr. J. B. Rhine of Duke University concluded that Lady Wonder read their thoughts using extrasensory perception (ESP).

Did the horse get the correct answers and make predictions by reading other people's minds? Is it possible that Lady Wonder used her own intelligence and reasoning processes to come up with the correct answers and predictions?

In the case of Morey Bernstein's luggage, no one knew where the bags were, so telepathy wouldn't have helped the horse locate them. Apparently, Lady was clairvoyant—able to locate missing objects or people by using special abilities beyond the normal five senses. By correctly predicting the outcomes of elections and sporting events, Lady Wonder showed that she also had the power of precognition—knowledge of events before they actually happen.

For nearly three decades, this amazing horse performed remarkable feats that could be explained only in terms of ESP and other paranormal phenomena. After a long and successful career, Lady Wonder had a heart attack and died on March 19, 1957.

King

The Carlsons rescued King one snowy Christmas Eve in 1975. The half German shepherd, half husky pup had apparently been abandoned by his owner. He had been left for dead with a bullet wound in his head. Nursed back to health by the Carlsons, the dog became "king" of the Carlson farm in Granite Falls, Washington.

Five years later, at Christmastime, a fire broke out in the Carlsons' kitchen at about 3:30 in the morning. Everyone was sound asleep. Suddenly, King ran into seventeen-year-old Pearl Carlson's bedroom, grabbed hold of her arm, and pulled her out of bed. Awake now, Pearl saw the thick black smoke spreading through the house. "Fire!" she screamed. "The house is on fire!"

Fern Carlson woke up quickly and led her ill husband, Howard, to the bedroom window of their one-story house. "Jump outside," she said. Then Fern went to find her daughter and guided her to a window. They both escaped.

Hearing a whining sound coming from the burning house, Fern realized King was still inside. "Come, King," she commanded the dog. But instead of jumping outside, the animal ran deeper into the house.

Immediately, Fern understood King's strange behavior. Her husband must still be inside! Fern climbed back through the window into the house, and King led her to Howard, who had collapsed on the floor. With great difficulty, Fern managed to break open a window, and she and Howard jumped to safety. King refused to move until all of the Carlsons were safe.

The house burned to the ground, but everyone was okay. King's hair was scorched by the fire, and the pads of his feet were burned and swollen. His metal collar had become so hot from the flames that it seared the flesh around the dog's neck.

King saved the lives of the Carlsons that night, but no one knew how he had gotten into the house to warn Pearl. He slept in the recreation room off the kitchen, but the door into the house had been closed.

When King refused to eat after the fire, the Carlsons discovered that he had long, painful wood splinters in his mouth and jaw. To save his beloved family, King had frantically chewed through the wooden kitchen door to get into the house to sound the alarm. It's no wonder that King was named the Ken-L Ration Dog Hero of the Year in 1981!

What powers of intelligence, reasoning, and loyalty did this animal possess to risk his own life to save others? When the way into the house was blocked, the dog could have easily escaped through the pet door into the backyard. Yet he chose to chew through the kitchen door, enduring much pain, to get into the house.

Was it merely instinct that governed the actions of King and led him to save his family? Or was it something more, a mystery that cannot be explained within the normal understanding of the abilities of animals?

Bloodsuckers

It was a warm summer night. The young woman tossed and turned restlessly in her sleep. The second-floor balcony doors had been left open to let in the night air.

Scattered clouds covered the face of the full moon. A slight breeze ruffled the window drapery. Only the sounds of hooting owls and other nocturnal creatures could be heard.

Suddenly, a large, black-winged bat flew through the open balcony doors and circled above the bed of the sleeping woman. The clock chimed midnight as the bat changed into a human male figure dressed entirely in black. As he bent over the sleeping form, the man pulled back his lips to reveal large canine-type fangs.

As the fangs of the dreaded vampire pierced the throat of the young woman, she moaned aloud, but she did not awaken. The creature feasted on the woman's blood. When the vampire was satisfied, it changed back into a bat and flew out into the night.

The young victim awoke the next morning feeling even more tired than when she went to sleep. She looked pale and unhealthy and wondered to herself, "What are those two small marks on my neck?"

This is a typical scene from one of those old late-night vampire movies starring Bela Lugosi. But everyone knows there are no such things as vampires—or are there? Except for the part where the bat turns into a man and then back into a bat again, this scene could have really happened! Vampire bats do exist and have been known to drink the blood of unsuspecting people!

There are nearly one thousand species of bats, but only three live exclusively on blood. In fact, their throats are too small to swallow anything else. Two bat species feed on the blood of birds, but the third feasts on cattle, horses, and sometimes even humans!

The small, brown vampire bat has a mouth full of razor-sharp teeth. It uses its

two upper center teeth (called incisors) to puncture the skin. Instead of sucking the blood, as vampires supposedly do, the vampire bat laps it up with its tongue from the wound of its unfortunate victim.

A chemical in the bat's saliva contains an anticoagulant that allows the blood to keep flowing by not allowing it to clot. The vampire bat will feed for twenty to twenty-five minutes before it is full. Strangely enough, its victims are unaware they have been bitten by these creatures, although loss of blood can cause weakness and lower resistance to disease.

The main danger in the bite of a vampire bat is that it may carry rabies, a disease that can be deadly to people and other animals. Vampire bats are found in South and Central America. They sleep during the day and feed only at night.

Nearly all legends have some basis in fact. It's not a coincidence that vampire stories and bats are connected with one another. One need only learn a little about the very real and unusual vampire bat to discover one of the strangest mysteries of nature.

The Killer Sea Wasp

It was a beautiful day to be at the beach. The sun was shining, and the sky was bright blue and cloudless. The water was warm and clear.

Thousands of sunbathers flocked to the beaches near North Queensland, Australia, to relax, get some color in their cheeks, and have fun. Families spread blankets on the sand and distributed food and drink to adults and children.

The toddlers and younger children, under the watchful gaze of parents, played in the wet sand near the water. The older children waded into the shallows.

An eleven-year-old girl waved to her

mother, who was sitting on a blanket. The girl was about fifty feet from shore, in water that barely reached her knees. The girl never saw the colorless, bell-shaped body of the jellyfish as her legs brushed against it in the water. Had she seen this particular species, called the sea wasp, she might have thought it to be quite beautiful and fragile-looking.

From the exact moment the girl's legs touched the trailing tentacles of the jellyfish, all she was aware of was a terrible burning pain. Then she collapsed into unconsciousness. By the time other bathers carried the girl to shore, she was dead, a victim of one of the most deadly creatures on earth.

An autopsy of the girl's body revealed that her lungs and respiratory system were congested and filled with mucus. Marks on her legs showed numerous tentacle stings.

Some people believe this girl was one of the lucky ones. Unconsciousness and death in less than a minute are preferable to the usual symptoms of sea wasp victims. These symptoms include agonizing pain, blindness, muscle spasms, sweating, and shortness of breath for minutes and possibly hours before eventual heart failure and death.

If the unfortunate victim is stung in deeper water, he or she may drown before

getting to shore. It is believed that many drowning deaths in northern Australia are actually the result of sea wasp stings.

The body of the sea wasp ranges from about two to eight inches across and is four to five inches wide. It's made up mostly of water and is clear in color. As many as fifty tentacles trail away from the corners of the body, sometimes reaching lengths of up to four feet.

Each tentacle has thousands of tiny stinging cells called nematocysts. Each nematocyst injects venom into the unfortunate victim like a doctor injects medicine in a hypodermic needle into a patient's arm.

The sea wasp uses its tentacles to locate food and as a self-defense mechanism. They're often found in shallow water close to shore, searching for bottom-dwelling shrimp to eat. Sea wasps live in the waters around Australia, the Bahamas, Brazil, the Philippines, and even the south Atlantic coast of the United States.

The venom of this deadly creature is believed to be the strongest, most potent that exists in nature. It's no wonder that sea wasps are more feared than sharks or cobras! Although other jellyfish stings are treatable, there is no way to counteract the venom of the sea wasp.

Until scientists solve the problem of discovering an antidote, the sea wasp will continue to threaten beach lovers and swimmers with its painful sting of death. The fact is, even if an antidote is someday found, there may not be enough time to use it!

Sam's Journey

When Debbie and Ray Foltz moved from Montrose, Colorado, to Santee, California, in 1983, they had to make an important decision. They couldn't take both their dogs with them.

With two pets, Debbie and Ray were afraid nobody would rent them a home. They decided to leave Sam, their one-year-old Yorkshire terrier–poodle mix, with a friend in Montrose. Sam's mother, the other dog, traveled to California with the Foltz family.

Sam missed his family so much that one night he left his new home in Montrose and began an amazing journey. The little dog traveled on foot through four states and across 840 miles. No one knows how he did it, but one day a dirty, exhausted, and hungry Sam turned up outside the door of the new Foltz home in Santee!

Debbie and Ray could hardly believe it was the dog they had left behind. "Walking here is the only way he could have made it," said Debbie. "His paws were all worn and hurt. He was suffering from malnutrition and muscle spasms when he showed up at our door."

Right away, Sam's mother went to work licking and cleaning her son. Debbie and Ray took the little dog to the veterinarian, who tended to his wounds. Sam was his old self in a few days.

"I don't know how he managed to find us. It's just one of those miracles you hear about," explained Debbie.

What makes Sam's journey so incredible is not the fact that the dog was so small and the distance so far. Rather, it was the fact that Sam had no idea where the family was headed. How could he have known where they were moving? How could he have known which direction to travel?

The tiny terrier walked out of Colorado, possibly into Utah or New Mexico, through Arizona, the Mojave Desert, and then to Santee in Southern California. Finally, he managed to locate the exact house of the Foltz family. How did he do it? How did Sam seek out and find his owners?

Scientists don't really know how dogs can travel through strange cities, over highways, and even across mountains and rivers they have never seen before. Some call it "the homing instinct," although there's no proof that it is an instinct. Others say it's a type of extrasensory perception called psi-trailing or "orientation by unexplained means."

There is no way to know how Sam endured the physical part of the journey in addition to following the trail of the Foltz family. Did the terrier share a psychic bond with Debbie and Ray? Did he read their minds, following their route and location?

Science cannot explain this phenomenon, and the mystery remains unsolved.

The Archerfish

The leafy plants that hang over the banks of the small streams in Southeast Asia are populated with many insects and spiders. Inches above the surface of the water, the small creatures are unaware that they are being stalked.

The danger comes from the water below. A fish swims near the surface of the stream, then stops directly below a small spider resting on some vegetation. The spider is more than six inches above the fish, whose eyes seem to focus directly on the small creature.

The fish's mouth breaks the surface, opens slightly, and suddenly spits several drops of water directly at the spider. The insect is hit, falls into the stream, and is immediately eaten by the fish, called the archerfish.

The unusual archerfish has the unique ability to shoot down insects above the surface of the water. It grows up to twelve inches in length and is found mainly in waters of the South Pacific and Southeast Asia.

Although much of its food consists of shrimp, insect larvae, and other small water creatures, the archerfish prefers to eat the live food it stalks and shoots. Occasionally it can bring down flying insects, not just those at rest.

The shape of the fish's mouth gives it the ability to shoot a stream of water as a weapon. There is a groove in the roof of the mouth that, when the tongue presses upward against the groove, forms a narrow tube. The water is then driven through the tube when the gill covers are closed.

An adult archerfish can accurately hit insects with a stream of water up to six feet or more above the surface! On the rare occasion when the fish misses its mark, the aim is adjusted and other shots quickly follow.

The force of the water spit by an archerfish can knock an insect high in the air. People who have been hit by the stream have said the water stung their face.

The mystery of the archerfish revolves

around the question of intelligence. Some believe its eyes are more advanced than other fish, allowing them to focus and judge distance accurately. Others point to the fact that their aim can be adjusted and improved, showing that it's more of a learned ability.

An example of this type of ability took place in an aquarium exhibit of 150 archerfish in a large tank. According to Maurice and Robert Burton, in the *Encyclopedia of Fish*, at feeding time the water level was lowered and small bits of hamburger meat were thrown against the sides of the tank above the surface of the water. The fish started to spit water at the meat. Within minutes, much of the hamburger washed down from the sides of the tank into the mouths of the hungry archerfish.

In *Strangest Creatures on Earth*, Edward M. Weyer, Jr., wrote about a friend in Thailand who entertained guests with special performances of archerfish. His balcony was directly over the water, and the fish would congregate each day and wait for small food scraps to be thrown to them. When a spider or cricket was tied by a thread to a pole and lowered to several feet above the water, the archerfish exhibited their shooting skills as they tried to catch their meal.

Weyer noted that on two separate occasions the fish put out his friend's cigarette while he sat reading a newspaper!

Is it instinct that causes the archerfish to shoot accurately at its targets, or is it intelligence that directs its actions? Scientists don't know.

The "Bomber" Beetle

The bird was gathering insects to feed her young when it spotted the ground beetle under a rock. The beetle's body was a bright orange-tan color with blue-black wing covers. It was small and looked harmless, and the bird thought it might be a tasty treat.

As the bird bent to pick up the insect, there was a loud popping sound. A foul-smelling stinging fluid spurted out of the beetle, hitting the bird right in the face. It squawked in pain and surprise and dropped the beetle instantly. The bird's eyes were burning as it flew quickly away. Never again would it bother another bombardier beetle!

Just as the bombardier on military aircraft dropped bombs of destruction on wartime targets, the bombardier beetle shoots bombs of burning chemicals on its enemies. Whenever it is attacked or threatened, the beetle's rear end turns into a cannon, firing up to twenty-nine shots in succession before resting and refueling if necessary.

Scientists have found that the mixture of chemicals that make up these "beetle bombs" is boiling hot and can cause an angry red welt on human skin.

The firepower of the bombardier beetle comes from two glands in its abdomen. Several chemicals are stored within the glands. When mixed together, they create a powerful reaction that causes the compound to shoot from the beetle's body. This mixture has been described as a "hot, stinging spray."

The bombardier beetle is just one of nearly 250,000 species of beetles, ranging in size from a hundredth of an inch to more than eight inches in length. The beetles' tough, hard outer bodies are so strong, they can carry loads one thousand times their own weight!

There are endless varieties of beetles. One type eats the lead covering on telephone cables, while another eats grain. Still others bury small dead animals underground to eat at a later date. The most popular and useful

of beetles are ladybugs, which help farmers by eating aphids and other insects that attack fruit crops.

Bombardier beetles are half an inch long and live mainly in tropical and subtropical climates throughout the world. They are common carnivorous (meat-eating) beetles, and they rest during the day and hunt for food during the night.

The mystery of the bombardier beetle isn't the unique method of self-defense it uses against enemies, including large ants, reptiles, and birds. Rather, the mystery is how this small insect can store and use such acidic chemicals without being burned or injured.

Scientists think that the secret lies in the beetle's hard outer skeleton of armor, called the chitin, which seems to be used especially for this protective purpose. Until the answer is clear, scientists will continue to study this problem. The bombardier's body is unique in that it can store and use acidic chemicals without injury. The question is, how?

Giants of the Deep

The octopus has a bad reputation. Many people believe it's a giant long-armed monster that lives in the depths of the ocean. It eagerly waits to kill divers and drag ships to a watery grave. That's how author Jules Verne described the creature that attacked the submarine *Nautilus* in *20,000 Leagues Under the Sea*.

Incidents like the one described above are likely to apply to the giant squid, which is more aggressive than the usually timid octopus. A squid will attack prey with its ten long arms and then tear it apart with its sharp and powerful beak. One giant squid measured fifty-seven feet, including thirty-five-foot-long tentacles!

The squid's main enemy is the sperm whale. At about sixty feet long, it's one of the largest creatures in the world. The two often battle to the death. Large tentacle marks on the bodies of captured sperm whales indicate they were attacked by giant squids at least two hundred feet long! Although a squid of this size has never actually been seen by man, it is believed to exist in the unexplored depths of the ocean.

In contrast to the squid, an octopus is a loner by nature and will generally avoid confrontation. It has eight, not ten, tentacles and changes color to blend into its surroundings when threatened or afraid. It can stretch and flatten itself to slip through the smallest of spaces. Some large octopuses measure thirty feet across, including tentacles, and most are very shy. They move slowly over the ocean's bottom, while the squid moves quickly through the water pursuing its prey.

Scientists have admitted the existence of the giant squid, but they are hesitant about supporting the existence of a species of giant octopuses, even though one specimen has already been identified.

It all started one day in November of 1896, nearly one hundred years ago. Two boys were bicycling on Anastasia Beach near Saint Augustine, Florida. Quite by accident they came upon what was later called "The Florida Monster."

They parked their bikes to investigate a huge carcass half buried in the sand. When they saw its enormous size, the two boys quickly went for help, and Dr. DeWitt Webb of Saint Augustine was called in. He concluded that the body was that of a large whale that had washed up on the beach. After closer examination, armlike extensions thirty-two feet long were found under the sand. The main body of the creature was twenty-three feet long and eighteen feet wide.

Webb believed he had found the body of a giant octopus and notified Professor Verrill of Yale University. In the meantime, he cut and preserved tissue samples from the specimen.

Without seeing the carcass, Verrill first decided it was a squid. After looking over photographs and other information, he changed his mind and said it was an octopus. Then, after examining tissue samples, he finally concluded the creature was a whale after all. At no time did Verrill ever examine the actual remains of the creature.

Many years passed. In 1957, Forrest Wood, a marine biologist, became interested in "The Florida Monster." Wood discovered that the Smithsonian Institution in Washington, D.C., had kept the tissue samples. With the help of his friend, Joseph Gennaro, Wood examined the samples and compared them with octopus and squid tissue. Gennaro concluded that the tissues were *not* from a whale or squid, but were similar to existing octopuses. "The Florida Monster" was actually a giant octopus (*Octopus giganteus*)!

Wood calculated that the huge creature must have measured more than 180 feet in length with the tentacles extended when it was alive! Many experts believe that species of giant octopuses live in the deepest part of the Atlantic Ocean—the Puerto Rico Trench, 27,498 feet deep.

Although scientists have been unable to find additional evidence to support the existence of the giant octopus, that doesn't mean this huge creature isn't hidden in the ocean's depths. Until deep exploration dives for long periods of time are commonplace, the sea will continue to hide its mysterious secrets and the amazing creatures lurking within it.

Sparky

Sparky, a 130-pound yellow Labrador retriever, loved going on walks with his master, John Culbertson. The early morning walk the big Lab took with his owner in January 1992 started out like all others in the six years they had been together. It was a cold winter day in Tullahoma, Tennessee, and although Sparky would have preferred to run and explore, he kept pace with his owner.

After the two had gone a short distance, Sparky sensed that something was wrong. Culbertson had stopped and seemed to be in distress. Suddenly, without warning, the big man became faint and collapsed to the ground. Before losing consciousness completely, he managed to slip his hand under Sparky's collar.

The yellow Lab couldn't wake up his owner. He licked his face and nudged him with his muzzle, but Culbertson didn't respond. Sparky realized that his master was in serious trouble. He decided to drag him home to get help. This was no easy task for the dog. His owner was a big man who weighed 227 pounds, an incredibly heavy weight for a dog to move.

Turning his body backward so the weight wouldn't pull at his chain collar and choke him, Sparky started dragging Culbertson home. Slowly but surely the Lab dragged his owner nearly two hundred yards to the front door of his house. He completed this difficult task just as Dorothy Culbertson stepped outside to look for her husband.

Seeing the exhausted dog and her unconscious husband, Dorothy immediately called an ambulance. Her fears were confirmed when doctors notified her that Culbertson had suffered a heart attack. Sparky's actions followed by immediate medical treatment probably saved his life.

John Culbertson later underwent triple bypass heart surgery and recovered from his heart attack. At his side was his faithful dog, Sparky.

"He saved my life, and he's worth millions to me," said Culbertson. "He's more of a friend than anything, and I will never never part with him."

Even as a frisky young pup, Sparky was special. He was raised by a neighbor, who also had a pet orangutan. When Culbertson developed a special attachment to the yellow Lab, his neighbor gave him the dog. Now the two are inseparable.

Sparky was named the Ken-L Ration Dog Hero of the Year for 1992. He received a certificate of merit, an engraved bowl, and a year's supply of Kibbles'n'Bits dog food. But what Sparky really cared about most was a pat and rub on the head from his master.

A special and mysterious bond exists between dogs and their owners. Loyalty, courage, and devotion are adjectives attributed more often to dogs than to any other creature.

Few would argue that the dog feels a wide range of emotions—from grief to anger to love. Many believe that the dog's attachment to humans is so strong it even exceeds the animal's own instinct for survival.

Man-Eating Plants

The trunk of the strange tree looked like an eight-foot-high pineapple sitting on its base. It was dark brown in color, and giant leaves attached at the top hung down to the ground. These huge leaves were thick and wide, and their outer surface was covered with sharp, hooked thorns.

A hole in the top of the tree was filled with a mysterious sweet liquid. Many hairy tendrils, which looked like the arms of an octopus, stretched out from the top in all directions but were motionless.

The natives surrounded the tree and forced one of their women to climb the leaves and stand at the peak. As the woman drank some of the liquid, the tree suddenly came to life. The green tendrils, one by one, wrapped their arms around her body, neck, and limbs. Like a nightmarish monster, the tendrils tightened their grip and strangled the life from their victim.

The woman's screams were reduced to quiet moans and then silence. As the giant leaves rose slowly in the air and enveloped her body, blood and fluid trickled down the trunk of the monstrous tree. The natives danced and cheered at the sight and drank the awful mixture. Ten days later, the leaves came down and nothing was left of the unfortunate woman except a skull at the foot of the tree.

Was this a scene from *Little Shop of Horrors*, the musical about a man-eating plant? Perhaps it was a clip from a late-night grade B horror movie? Guess again.

Based on an eyewitness description of a man-eating tree in Madagascar, which is an island off the coast of southeastern Africa, the incident was described in a letter written by Carle Liche, a German tourist. The letter was published in European scientific journals, magazines, and newspapers in the 1870s and 1880s.

Does this tree really exist? Many scientists believe it was a figment of the writer's

imagination. Though no specimen has been discovered supporting the existence of a man-eating tree, natives of Madagascar tell stories about the tree's existence. In fact, the belief in a man-eating tree or plant is common in southern Asia, including India.

Meat-eating plants do exist in nature. One example is the well-known Venus's flytrap, which feeds on the nutrients (mainly nitrogen) it gets from digesting insects. Its open leaves reveal a red center that secretes a liquid that smells like nectar. Insects are attracted to the color and smell.

Once the victim touches two of the sensitive trigger hairs, the open leaves flap shut and trap the prey inside. Digestive fluids slowly kill and dissolve the insect, and the flaps open again in a few days.

The Venus's flytrap is found mainly in North and South Carolina, and it feeds mostly on ants or flies. It will eat all meat and is capable of trapping and digesting even small frogs.

Another meat-eater is the pitcher plant, found in the southeastern part of the United States. Insects, attracted by the smell of nectar, stray into the pitcher-shaped hollow leaves of the plant. Thin hairs on the inside walls cause the insect to slip farther down into the hollow center until it reaches fluid at the bottom. There it drowns and begins to be digested by the plant.

Carnivorous, or meat-eating, plants are a unique and fascinating part of nature. Most people believe, however, that *man*-eating plants exist only in myths and stories. No one knows for sure. There are still many unexplored regions of the world, and these may yet reveal incredible, previously unknown mysteries.

Electric Eel

The local people of Calabozo, a small town in Venezuela, South America, had prepared a surprise for their guest. It was at the turn of the century, in the year 1800. The German scientist Baron von Humboldt was interested in the strange eels, native to the area, that produced electric current.

The townspeople were determined to provide von Humboldt with a live demonstration, along with some specimens. Although they didn't understand what electricity was, they knew this eel caused pain to animals and humans when they swam too close to it.

The locals herded several dozen horses into the swampland pools where the eels lived. The horses panicked and disturbed the eels, who started sending out electrical currents through the water.

Von Humboldt watched in fascination as some of the horses were stunned so badly they fell to their knees or drowned. The natives were able to capture several eels, which von Humboldt examined in detail and then later dissected.

The German scientist wanted to experience the electrical power of the eels firsthand, so he stood on the body of a live specimen. All at once, he felt a numbing pain throughout his body and then intense pain in his knees and joints as the eel shocked him.

Von Humboldt was responsible for the very first scientific account of the behavior of the electric eel. Well ahead of his time, he predicted that "electricity is the source of life and movement in all living things."

The electric eel has a thick, rounded body that ranges from six feet to about ten feet in length. Its eyes are very small, and one writer described its appearance as "looking like a child's unfinished clay animal." It lives in the swampy regions of northern South America.

The internal organs of the eel are contained in an area behind the head. The tail

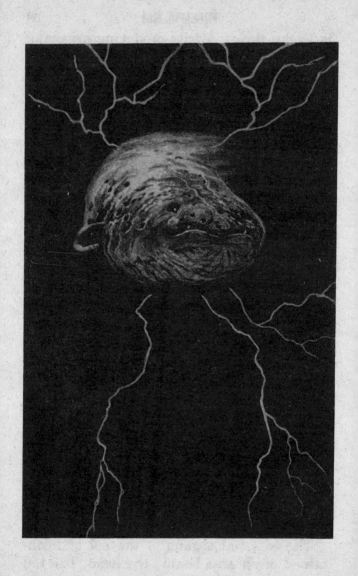

is where the electricity-producing organs of the eel are located. The tail is made up of thousands of sections, similar to cells in a battery. Just as any battery has a negative and positive end, the electric eel's head is positive, while the tail end is negative.

As the eel swims through the water, it sends out continuous weak electrical impulses. These impulses help guide it around obstacles and can also detect nearby prey. The eel uses its high-voltage capabilities to kill prey and for self-defense.

This amazing creature is capable of discharging up to six hundred volts at a time. That's enough power to light a dozen household bulbs! These high-voltage discharges can kill small fish and animals that the eel eats, and can stun large animals and even human beings. The danger to man lies in the possibility of drowning after being shocked.

Other species of electric fish include the electric catfish and the electric ray.

Nancy

Most incidents involving animals with mysterious and unexplained powers occur among household pets. Yet wild animals have also performed remarkable feats of extrasensory perception and intelligence. Take the case of a sea gull named Nancy described in the book *Psychic Animals* by Dennis Bardens.

Rachel Flynn and her sister, June, lived in Cape Cod, Massachusetts. Their home was a mile away from the ocean, and Rachel loved to walk on the rocky beaches and take in the beautiful New England scenery.

The two elderly sisters befriended one of the many sea gulls in the area. They fed it

regularly and named the gull Nancy. Rachel
and June looked forward to their daily visits
with Nancy, and the bird seemed to return
their friendship.

One day eighty-two-year-old Rachel was
walking alone along the cliffs overlooking
the ocean when she tripped and fell. She
tumbled thirty feet down an embankment
and landed on the beach below. She couldn't
move and realized she must be seriously injured. Even worse, she lay trapped between
two large rocks and wasn't easily visible
from the cliff.

Thinking she would surely die, Rachel
suddenly spotted a sea gull fluttering in the
air above her.

Could it be Nancy? she thought. *Sea gulls
all look alike, yet this one seems to be purposely staying near me.*

Out loud Rachel said, "For God's sake,
Nancy, get help! Go! Get help!"

Sure enough, the bird flew away. "I probably scared it off," mumbled Rachel, who was
in great pain by now, and she closed her eyes
to rest.

What Rachel didn't know was that the
bird flew directly to the Flynn house, where
June was working in the kitchen. Nancy
tapped on the window with her beak over
and over again and flapped her wings.

"Shoo, Nancy, go away," said June, but the sea gull continued tapping.

"Leave, you silly bird," June snapped. "Don't bother me!"

After nearly fifteen minutes, June realized that the bird was trying to communicate with her. She went outside and said loudly, "What do you want, Nancy?" The gull flew a short distance and then stopped to be sure June would follow. The elderly woman walked as quickly as she could to try to keep up with the sea gull. She was a little frightened now because she hadn't seen Rachel in quite some time. June wondered if the gull's visit had something to do with her sister.

At last Nancy set down on the edge of the cliff. When June looked over, she searched the beach carefully and finally spotted her sister trapped below. "I'll get help, Rachel," she shouted down. "I'll be back soon. Hang on."

Rachel was hospitalized with an injured knee and severe cuts and bruises. June was positive that the bird had saved her sister's life.

How did the sea gull know Rachel needed help? It's too much of a coincidence for the bird to be flying in the exact location that the accident occurred. Did Nancy sense Rachel's distress and then fly to the scene?

What reasoning and thought processes did the bird use to fly back to the Flynn house and summon June by tapping on the window? What type of intelligent creature led the woman to her sister so she could get help?

When people use the term "birdbrain," they're referring to those with limited intelligence skills. Many scientists believe that birds are not capable of higher thoughts and reasoning. But don't tell that to Rachel Flynn, who owes her life to a birdbrain named Nancy.

Sea Serpents and Lake Monsters

It is a fact that large, mysterious, and unidentified animals live in the underwater depths of the world's lakes and oceans. The Loch Ness monster of Loch Ness in Scotland is the most famous.

For lack of a better name, this creature has been called a sea serpent or lake monster. For hundreds of years, men, women, and children have reported seeing it.

"It had a large, sharp snout and broad, large flippers," said a 1734 sighting.

"A great head and long neck rose out of the water . . . it had a series of humps," reported one 1905 sighting.

A 1915 sighting said, "It was about sixty

feet long ... and had four powerful paddle-like limbs."

A 1961 sighting stated, "We saw three humps, each about six feet long, and two near-side flippers come out of the water in a paddling motion."

"The creature was about seventy feet long. The head was large, the skin a dull brownish black in color," reported a sighting from 1965.

Descriptions often vary in the great number of reported sightings throughout the world. Yet there are several obvious similarities. This creature seems to be very large and has a long neck and flippers.

Some scientists have suggested this animal might be a giant eel or snake. But eels and snakes don't have the long neck or flippers reported in many sightings. Others insist it is a variety of long-neck seal or otter.

In another part of the world, in 1977, a Japanese trawler off the coast of New Zealand discovered the body of a thirty-foot-long creature in its nets. It had a long neck, four flippers, and weighed about four thousand pounds. The fisherman photographed, sketched, and measured the creature. Because it smelled so bad and was decomposing, the crew thought their catch of fresh fish would be spoiled. Unfortunately, they

threw the body back into the sea, thus depriving scientists of the chance to identify the creature.

From the photos and sketches, Japanese scientists concluded that it could have been a plesiosaur, a marine reptile extinct for 60 to 100 million years! Is it possible? After all, the prehistoric fish coelacanth, also thought to be extinct, was discovered alive and well in waters off southern Africa.

The Japanese scientists later changed their minds and concluded that the creature was the remains of a large basking shark. Without physical evidence, however, it's impossible to know for sure.

Many in the scientific community believe the plesiosaur is the answer to the reported sightings of sea serpents and lake monsters throughout the world. The plesiosaur had a long snakelike neck, a broad solid body, and four paddlelike legs. It ranged in size from ten to sixty feet.

The problem is, the plesiosaur was a saltwater reptile, and many of the sightings were made in very cold freshwater lakes. One theory states that long ago these areas were once part of the oceans that covered much of the Earth. Over the years, the water receded and the land emerged to cut off the lakes and trap the creatures within them from the sea.

The water changed slowly over time from salt to fresh, just as the temperatures changed from mild to very cold. The trapped plesiosaurs adapted slowly to these changes and still live in the depths today, coming to the surface occasionally.

Whatever they are, it is possible that these animals do exist. So many people have testified to their existence that it is almost impossible to pass them off as the result of an overactive imagination.

Are they giant eels, snakes, or seals? Are they living prehistoric reptiles from the Age of Dinosaurs? Are they serpents or monsters? Until a physical specimen is discovered and examined, the world can only wait and wonder.

Cunning Crows

The crows barely took notice of the farmer who waved his arms and tried to scare them away. The more the birds munched on the wheat, the more upset and frustrated the farmer became. He was determined not to let the crows destroy the crop that had taken him so long to grow.

The farmer hurried to his truck, reached for the rifle he kept under the seat, and mumbled out loud, "It's time to do a little crow hunting." As he got out of the truck, rifle in hand, and approached the birds, they spread their wings and took off instantly. It was as if the crows had warned each other, "He's got a gun now, let's get out of here."

The farmer scratched his head, got back into the truck, and drove off. Within minutes, the crows were back, eating the wheat as if nothing had happened.

This is a familiar scene to many farmers. Crows are considered to be the most intelligent of all birds. Were they reacting to the presence of the rifle itself or to the farmer's attitude, which changed once he got the rifle? It's difficult to determine the answer.

According to Jean Craighead George's book *Beastly Inventions*, a man named E. R. Kalmbach conducted an interesting experiment. He dressed in a long skirt and floppy hat that covered his face. Next, he hid a rifle in a hollow broomstick.

When Kalmbach got out of his car to face the crows, broomstick in hand, they flew away immediately. Later, he dressed exactly the same way but carried the broomstick without the rifle. Not only did he get out of his car, but he walked into the field. The crows didn't give him a second glance. They continued eating.

How did the crows know whether Kalmbach was armed and dangerous? Although birds possess the five senses of sight, hearing, touch, taste, and smell, their sense of sight has developed to a much greater degree than it has in other animals.

Could the crow's keen sense of sight have detected the rifle in the broomstick? That seems highly unlikely since no part of it was visible at any time. It's possible that the bird's sharp eyesight might have noticed certain movements of aggression and anger in the man that the crows recognized as danger.

Kalmbach was not consciously aware of changes in his body movements with or without the rifle. Yet, when he walked into the field with the weapon hidden in the broomstick, he was mentally thinking, "I'm going to kill some crows." This attitude might have caused minor changes in his walk and body movements that the crows were able to immediately sense.

If it wasn't the sharp eyesight of the crows that detected danger, was it something else that cannot be explained within the normal boundaries of the five senses? Could the crows have used ESP to determine if they were in danger?

Buffy

"I think we've found a beautiful spot to camp, Buffy," declared Mary Kearns to her pet keeshond. She chose a campsite in the valley near a small stream. It was an isolated clearing surrounded by small trees and bushes.

As Mary parked the car and began to unpack, she commented to the dog, "It's really lovely here. I hope I remembered to bring my camera."

Suddenly, Buffy ran to Mary and began barking in an odd unsettling way. As Mary carried supplies from the car to the campsite, the dog became more and more agitated.

"Take it easy, Buffy. What's bothering you?" asked Mary as she tried to calm down the anxious animal. But Buffy would not quiet down. His barking became wild and almost frightening.

Mary began to wonder whether camping here was such a good idea after all. The dog certainly didn't like this spot. His behavior seemed so strange that Mary's doubts about the place also grew.

She knew Buffy was a special dog. He always seemed to know about things before they happened. She remembered how Buffy would bark and get excited before her daughter came to visit.

"Okay, Buffy, you win," declared Mary out loud to the keeshond. "I think it would be better if we found another place." Mary repacked the car and drove a distance until she located another pretty camping spot, this time on a hillside.

"I think this is an even lovelier spot than before," she exclaimed. "What a fabulous view of the area!" Buffy, who had completely calmed down, licked his owner's hand and curled up at her feet. After a good dinner and a short walk, Mary and Buffy settled down for the night.

Up early after a restful sleep, Mary broke camp, repacked her gear, and began traveling again. Passing through a nearby town, she bought a local paper and saw some shocking news. The headline read "THREE CAMPERS DROWNED IN FLASH FLOOD."

The newspaper article described how an unexpected rainstorm high in the mountains caused a flash flood. The water roared down a valley without warning, killing the unfortunate campers. It was the exact valley where she and Buffy had first stopped to camp!

How had Buffy known there was something wrong? Can animals sense danger before it happens? Did Buffy know he and his owner would be drowned in a flash flood if they camped in the valley that night? Or was it by chance that the keeshond became so upset?

A precognitive warning or a coincidence? Mary Kearns is convinced that Buffy's powers of extrasensory perception saved her life.

Spiders on the Loose

"It's an ugly bug. Kill it quickly!" screams a girl as a common household spider scurries across the carpet of her house. After it's crushed with a tissue and deposited in the garbage can, the girl heaves a sigh of relief. "Spiders are so creepy and disgusting! I hate them."

People fear and dislike spiders mainly because of the way they look and act. They have eight long legs, move fast, hide in dark corners, and spin sticky webs that trap bugs. They may not be lovable little creatures, but they control the number of insects in the house and garden. They're a benefit to mankind even if people don't appreciate them.

There are thirty thousand species of spiders in the world, some of which live fascinating lives. Just imagine the South American bird-eating spider. With a ten-inch leg span, it's the largest of them all!

One type of spider spends its entire life underwater, yet it still breathes oxygen. The water spider spins silk and attaches it to an underwater plant. Then the spider returns to the surface and traps an air bubble with its body. The bubble is released under the silk to form an air pocket shaped like a tiny bell. After several more trips to the surface for more air, the spider's home is complete. When the oxygen supply gets low, the spider rises again for more air.

The fishing or diving spider is comfortable on land as well as water. It walks or floats on the surface of the water using an air bubble held beneath its body. Resting on plant leaves, this spider dangles its front legs in the water. In this way, it attracts insects and, in some cases, very small fish and tadpoles to eat. When frightened, the fishing spider dives several inches beneath the surface and can stay underwater for up to an hour!

The web-throwing spider spins a net and holds it with its legs. The spider then hangs upside down from a plant or branch. It waits

for prey to pass underneath and casts the net on unsuspecting insects.

The bolas spider is named after the Spanish weapon used to lasso or rope cattle. A bola is a long cord or thong with heavy balls at the end. This spider manufactures its own special bola to catch prey.

The bolas attaches a single horizontal silk line to the bottom of a branch or twig. The spider then spins a second line that hangs down vertically from the first. At the end of the second line, the spider attaches a sticky gumlike substance in the shape of a small ball.

Hanging from the first line, the spider uses several of its legs to grasp and control the second line. Just as a cowboy might use a lasso or bola to snare cattle, this spider swings the line to catch insects. The spider aims carefully so the ball at the end of the line hits the prey and sticks to it. Before the unfortunate victim can free itself, the spider rushes in for the kill.

Of the thousands of species of spiders that exist, only about a dozen are really dangerous to man. Of these, the black widow is the best known. It only bites in self-defense but is capable of killing an animal thousands of times its size.

Scientists wonder why the small black

widow spider, which captures prey from its web, also possesses a bite more powerful than rattlesnake venom. It's actually more dangerous to male spiders than to people, for after mating, the black widow often eats the male!

Dolphins to
the Rescue

No woman had ever swum the fifteen-mile channel called Cook Strait in New Zealand. Lynne Cox, a long-distance swimmer, wanted to be the first. She knew it would be difficult, but she never expected it to be so dangerous.

It wasn't the distance that bothered her. When Lynne was fourteen, she swam from the California coast to Catalina Island, twenty-seven miles in all. It took her twelve hours and thirty-six minutes under good weather conditions and in a calm sea.

Swimming through Cook Strait was a little like traveling through a hurricane. The winds were up to forty-five knots and the waves were six to eight feet high. The boat that always accompanied Lynne on her swims was having trouble just staying afloat.

Lynne was getting very tired fighting the waves and weather. Despite shouts of encouragement from her trainer in the boat, the cold and exhaustion finally got to her. Lynne felt she couldn't go any farther.

Suddenly, just as she was about to quit the swim and signal the boat to pick her up, Lynne found herself surrounded by forty to fifty dolphins. It was as if the dolphins wanted to help her keep going.

"I started feeling better," said Lynne, "and concentrated on watching the dolphins instead of my own tiredness and the weather. After an hour, they left and another group of dolphins joined me. They were squeaking and clicking all around me. Some were so close that I could have reached out and touched them.

"The dolphins had perfect timing," Lynne explained. "They came when I was feeling bad and cheered me up. It was wonderful." She adds, "They guided me right in to the finish!"

Did the dolphins sense that Lynne was in trouble and about to give up? Did they purposely swim with her, or was it just a coincidence that they came at that particular moment?

Some people think that dolphins are not only extremely intelligent creatures but have a special psychic ability beyond the normal five senses. Most people agree that there is a unique link between dolphins and man. They have attacked sharks but they have never attacked people. In fact, there are numerous stories on record that dolphins have helped or rescued people from drowning.

In one report, a drowning woman was pushed to shore by a dolphin. Another swimmer was having trouble with muscle cramps. A dolphin swam up under him and kept him afloat until the cramps passed. Still another swimmer became disoriented and panicked in the water, unable to find his way back to his boat. A dolphin appeared to guide him out of trouble.

How could the dolphins know these people were in peril? And if the creatures sensed danger, how did they know what to do to solve the problem?

There are those who believe that dolphins

use telepathic ability to read people's minds. Others say they are friendly, intelligent, and playful animals who just happen to show up at the right time.

Is it a coincidence or telepathy? Someday scientists may discover the truth.

Forever Friends

Cats, more than other animals, are said to possess mysterious unexplained powers. Perhaps it's their independence and reserved nature that make people uncertain about cats—and in some cases, even afraid of them.

Whereas dogs are referred to as "man's best friend," cats are often seen as creatures of magic and the supernatural. They're portrayed unfairly by several commonly held beliefs and superstitions. It's said that witches take the form of black cats when they want to move freely and undetected among people. It's no coincidence that, at Halloween, black cat costumes and decorations are nearly as popular as ghosts and jack-o'-lanterns. This discomfort and uncertainty about felines have contributed to making the black cat a symbol of bad luck for superstitious people all year long!

Yet cats often have proven themselves to be just as faithful, obedient, and loyal as any other animal. Take the case of the cat named Bill. Bill and his owner shared a special relationship that only came from years of living together. They knew and understood each other's gestures, moods, habits, and body language.

One day, Bill was left at home while his master went on a short trip. It wasn't unusual for the cat to stay behind on these occasions. There was plenty of food, a litter box, and even a slightly open window so Bill could go in and out.

The days passed, and Bill's owner did not return home. He had been badly hurt in a train accident and died a few days later. The funeral took place in a cemetery near the hospital in which he had died.

The man's brother had made the funeral arrangements in a hurry. With everything else on his mind, he had completely forgotten about the cat. During the graveside service he was amazed to see Bill there. The cat had somehow known what had happened to his owner and traveled to the cemetery to pay his last respects to his beloved master.

After the service, the brother quietly watched as the cat walked slowly to the edge of the open grave and looked down at the coffin. After a few moments, Bill turned and slowly made his way home. There was no question in the brother's mind that the animal was suffering the loss of its master and friend.

Did the cat sense his owner's accident and death? How could Bill have known where the funeral was being held and when?

Whatever guided the cat to the funeral of his master, it's apparent Bill possessed two important qualities we all wish for in our animals as well as our friends—love and loyalty.

Chimp Talk

In the late 1960s, two teachers named Beatrix and Allen Gardner raised a young chimpanzee as if it were a human child. The Gardners did not believe that a chimp could imitate human speech, so they taught it sign language instead.

The chimp, named Washoe, eventually learned to use more than 132 signs. Dorothy Hinshaw Patent, in her book *How Smart Are Animals*, described how Washoe would sign "Baby mine" for her doll and "Listen dog" when a dog barked. She even invented her own new sign for the bib she wore.

Once Washoe asked one of her trainers, Roger Fouts, for some fruit. "Fruit me," she requested. Roger replied in sign language, "Sorry but I not have any fruit." Washoe wasn't pleased with this response and signed back "Dirty Roger." The chimp made up her own insult and used it to express her anger.

In another conversation with a human trainer, Washoe asked for an orange. When he replied, "No more orange, what you want?" the chimp again asked for an orange. When the trainer gave the same response, Washoe signed, "You go car gimme orange. Hurry!" The chimp remembered that people drove in cars to buy food at stores, although she hadn't been in one for two years.

There have been many successful language experiments with animals. In the 1970s a gorilla named Koko was taught over five hundred signs. Koko was able to make statements using three to six signs at once.

An orangutan named Chantek, in addition to knowing more than one hundred signs, learned to work for tokens to use toward rewards later on. If Chantek cleaned her room, she got a certain number of tokens and could exchange them for treats.

A pigmy chimpanzee named Kanzi was taught to communicate with symbols on a computer keyboard. He also learned to understand spoken English commands.

The question is, could these animals really

have understood language? It seemed so, yet scientists have expressed many doubts about these experiments. Some have said that when people are involved in reading signs made by chimps or gorillas, there is room for error in their interpretations. Perhaps unconsciously the people are interpreting a sign they want to see. Therefore, the success of these studies is difficult to judge.

Other scientists say the intention of the speaker is the key to understanding language. When a chimp signs "Orange," does it mean "I have a desire for an orange" or does it just know that the sign for orange will result in getting an orange? According to Dorothy Hinshaw Patent: "The difficult thing is finding out whether an animal is using symbols consciously or just performing behavior that will get rewards."

Didn't Washoe reveal an understanding and intelligence beyond that of simple memorization when she created her own word for her bib or made up an insult? Some scientists don't believe it does. They simply do not feel these animals have enough intelligence to put words together to form sentences or thoughts.

They point to the fact that few of the animals showed creativity in their language use. Whereas even a young child can enjoy stories and make up fantasies, these animals only spoke about real things they had contact with.

Such criticism of ape and chimp language research has led to large cuts in funding in this area. This is unfortunate, since there is much to be learned about the way animals think and feel and how they communicate with humans as well as other animals.

Someday we may discover whether animals can learn and understand human language. But there are those who would prefer not to know. As Patent states: "Perhaps it is difficult for some people to let go of the notion that language is the one thing that makes humans unique."

Strulli

"Let's go for a walk, Strulli," said Josef Becker to his German shepherd. According to Dennis Bardens, in his book *Psychic Animals*, the dog and master often went for a late afternoon stroll, usually ending up at the local inn. This particular day was no exception. Josef brought the dog inside with him, sat down, and ordered refreshments.

Josef began talking to some friends when suddenly the big dog started howling at his master. Strulli tugged at Josef's clothes and tried to drag him out of his seat. When Josef resisted, Strulli continued howling and started running around in circles.

"What is wrong with you today?" Josef

asked the usually well-behaved animal. "If you can't sit quietly, you'll have to leave!

"Back in a second, fellows," he said to his friends as he walked the dog outside, then ducked back into the inn, shutting the door behind him. "Now where was I?" asked Josef as he returned to his food and companions.

Within seconds, Strulli came through another open door and began tugging again at his master's clothes. "Looks like your dog doesn't want you to stay, Josef," said one of the men. "You won't have any peace with him carrying on like that."

"I'm sorry, boys," he apologized. "Something's bothering the dog, and I'll just have to find out what it is. I'll be back another time."

As Josef left the inn with Strulli, he glanced at his watch and saw that it was two minutes before five. They had barely been walking a couple of minutes when there was a deafening explosion behind him on the street.

Turning around, Josef was horrified to see that the inn had collapsed. Timber, bricks, and plaster had crashed down on the friends he had just left behind. Twenty people were injured and nine people were killed in the accident.

A shocked Josef turned slowly to face his

dog. "My god, Strulli, you knew, didn't you?" The man knelt down and held the pet close to him.

Did the German shepherd have a premonition of disaster? How could the dog have known something bad was going to happen? Not until much later was it discovered that builders next door had unknowingly damaged the inn's foundations, causing a weakening and the eventual collapse of the structure.

What special sensitivity and perception do dogs and other animals possess that enable them to have knowledge of future events? Too often, unexplained animal behavior is routinely ignored by calling it "instinct." Is it instinct to know the future or is it ESP? Do dogs have certain psychic abilities?

Next time your dog unexpectedly tugs at your clothing to get you to move, will you sit tight or will you follow? There's no doubt what Joséf Becker will do.

Glossary

AGGRESSION: attack, fight.

AGITATED: excited, frantic, wild.

ALKALOIDS: organic substances that contain nitrogen and can neutralize acids; some are very poisonous.

ANTICOAGULANT: stops blood from clotting.

APHID: an insect that sucks the juice from plants.

ASTEROID: small rocky objects in orbit around the sun.

ATTRIBUTE: belonging to, characteristic.

AUTOPSY: examination and dissection of a dead body to determine the cause of death.

BOMBARDIER: someone who operates a bomb sight and releases bombs.

CANINE: dog.
CARCASS: body, remains, corpse.
CARNIVOROUS: flesh- or meat-eating.
CHITIN: hard outer covering of insects.
CLAIRVOYANCE: the ability to identify or become aware of an object, person, or event without using the five basic senses (sight, hearing, smell, taste, and touch).
COINCIDENCE: occurrence or event that seems related to another but is not actually connected.
CONFIRM: approve, verify.
CONGESTED: clogged, overcrowded.
CRYPTOZOOLOGY: the study of hidden, unidentified living animals.
CURATOR: the person in charge of a museum, zoo, library, or other exhibit.

DEBRIS: wreckage, rubbish.
DECOMPOSE: decay, rot.
DISSECT: cut open, examine.
DISTRESS: difficulty, pain, anguish.

EMBANKMENT: rise or slope on a hillside.
EVENTUAL: expected, approaching.
EXCEED: go beyond, outdo, pass.
EXTINCT: dead, vanished.

EXTRASENSORY PERCEPTION (ESP): special abilities and knowledge that extend beyond the normal five senses.

FELINE: cat.
FEROCIOUS: violent, fierce.
FIGMENT: fantasy, made up.
FILLY: female horse, mare.
FLOUNDERING: struggling awkwardly.
FOSSIL: remains, skeleton.

GROOVE: slot, opening.
GUILLOTINE: a sharp-bladed machine used to cut off a person's head.

HERBIVOROUS: grass- or plant-eating.
HESITANT: unsure, reluctant.

IMITATE: copy, duplicate.
IMPULSE: a drive or force pushing a person or event forward.
INTERPRETATION: translation, explanation.

LARVA: an insect in the earliest stage of development.
LASSO: rope, snare.

MALNUTRITION: improper diet, undernourishment.
MAMMALS: human beings and animals that

feed mother's milk to their young and have skin covered with hair.

METEORITE: object from space, varying in size, that does not burn itself out in the Earth's atmosphere like a meteor but hits the Earth instead.

MUZZLE: snout, nose.

NEMATOCYST: stinging cells of jellyfish.

NOCTURNAL: active during the night.

NUDGE: gently push, shove.

PARANORMAL: not able to be explained by science.

PARASITE: a plant or animal that lives off another, giving nothing in return.

PENETRATE: enter, spread through.

PERCEPTION: understanding, awareness.

PERIL: danger, threat.

PHENOMENON: an extraordinary or unusual occurrence.

PHEROMONES: substances secreted by bees and other animals that change behavior; alarm pheromones make bees aggressive and attack in mass.

POLLINATION: transfer of pollen from the male to the female part of flowers and plants, which makes fruit and vegetable production possible.

POTENT: strong, powerful.

PRECOGNITION: the knowledge of events before they actually happen; the ability to see the future.

PREDATOR: an animal or person that destroys, robs, or eats greedily.

PREMONITION: an advance warning of an event; similar to precognition.

PREY: game, catch, target.

PRIMITIVE: crude, simple, ancient, from earliest times.

PSI-TRAILING: orientation by unexplained means.

PSYCHIC: sensitive to supernatural forces.

RECEDE: move back, withdraw.

REINCARNATION: the belief that a person's soul is reborn in a new bodily form after death.

ROE DEER: type of small European and Asiatic deer.

RUBBLE: wreckage, rubbish.

SCALES: outer protective covering of fish or reptiles.

SECRETE: ooze, drip.

SERRATED: sharp, sawlike notches on an edge.

SKEPTICAL: doubtful, uncertain.

SNARE: catch, trap, entangle.

SNOUT: nose, beak.

SPECIES: a single, distinct kind of plant or animal.

SPECIMEN: a sample.

SPORES: reproductive organs produced by mosses and ferns.

STALK: pursue or approach under cover.

SUCCESSION: in order, series.

SUPERNATURAL: anything caused by other than the known forces of nature.

SUPERSTITION: belief based on stories or myths, not necessarily true.

TELEPATHY: the ability to communicate over any distance from one mind to another without actually speaking.

TENDRILS: thin, armlike parts of a climbing plant that coil around or cling to something.

TENTACLES: long, thin, armlike extensions of octopus or squid used for grabbing or feeling.

TOKEN: similar to a coin that can be exchanged for something of value.

TRAWLER: a boat that drags along a large net to catch fish on the bottom.

UNIQUE: one of a kind, unequaled.

VENOM: poison.

Bibliography

Books

Allaby, Michael, and Lovelock, James. *The Great Extinction*. Garden City, N.Y.: Doubleday, 1983.

Bakker, Robert T. *The Dinosaur Heresies*. New York: William Morrow and Company, 1986.

Bardens, Dennis. *Psychic Animals*. New York: Henry Holt and Company, 1987.

Boone, J. Allen. *Kinship With All Life*. New York: Harper and Brothers, 1954.

Bronson, Wilfrid S. *Beetles*. New York: Harcourt, Brace and World, Inc., 1963.

Burton, Maurice, and Burton, Robert. *Encyclopedia of Fish*. London, Eng.: Octopus Books Limited, 1975.

Compton, Gail. "What Is the World's Deadliest Animal?" In *Maneaters and Marmosets*. New York: Hearst Books, 1976.

Constable, George. *Mysterious Creatures*. Richmond, Va.: Time-Life Books, 1988.

Cousteau, Jacques-Yves, and Diole', Philippe. *Octopus and Squid*. Garden City, N.Y.: Doubleday, 1973.

Dinsdale, Tim. *Monster Hunt*. Washington, D.C.: Acropolis Books, 1972.

Dozier, Thomas A. *Dangerous Sea Creatures*. New York: Time-Life Films, 1977.

George, Jean Craighead. *Beastly Inventions*. New York: David McKay Company, 1970.

Henry, Thomas R. *The Strangest Things in the World*. Washington, D.C.: Public Affairs Press, 1958.

Hitchings, Thomas, editor-in-chief. *Facts on File*. New York: Facts on File, Inc., 1991.

Jenkinson, Michael. *Beasts Beyond the Fire*. New York: E. P. Dutton, 1980.

Key, Alexander. *The Strange White Dove*. Philadelphia: Westminster Press, 1972.

Mackal, Roy P. *Searching for Hidden Animals*. Garden City, N.Y.: Doubleday, 1980.

Matthews, Rupert. *Monster Mysteries*. New York: The Bookwright Press, 1989.

Matthiessen, Peter. *Blue Meridian*. New York: Random House, 1971.

McFarland, Kevin. *Incredible!* New York: Hart Publishing Company, 1976.

Neary, John. *Insects and Spiders*. Richmond, Va.: Time-Life Books, 1977.

Patent, Dorothy Hinshaw. *How Smart Are Animals*. San Diego, Calif.: Harcourt Brace Jovanovich, Publishers, 1990.

Potter, Anthony. *The Killer Bees*. New York: Grosset and Dunlap, 1977.

Preston-Mafham, Rod, and Preston-Mafham, Ken. *Spiders of the World*. New York: Facts on File Publications, 1984.

Pringle, Laurence. *Batman—Exploring the World of Bats*. New York: Charles Scribner's Sons, 1991.

———*Killer Bees*. New York: Morrow Junior Books, 1990.

Reader's Digest Association. *Strange Stories, Amazing Facts*. Pleasantville, N.Y.: The Reader's Digest Association, Inc., 1976.

Steiger, Brad, and Steiger, Sherry Hansen. *Strange Powers of Pets*. New York: Donald I. Fine, 1992.

Stokes, Donald W. *A Guide to the Behavior of Common Birds*. Boston: Little, Brown and Company, 1979.

Taylor, David. *Animal Monsters*. Minneapolis, Minn.: Lerner Publications Company, 1989.

Thomson, Keith Stewart. *Living Fossil*. New York: W. W. Norton and Company, 1991.

Tributsch, Helmut. *When the Snakes Awake*. Cambridge, Mass.: The MIT Press, 1982.

Weyer, Edward M., Jr. *Strangest Creatures on Earth*. New York: Sheridan House, 1953.

Wylder, Joseph. *Psychic Pets*. New York: Stonehill Publishing, 1978.

Periodicals

"Sam's Incredible Journey of Love." *Weekly World News*. May 3, 1983.

"The Dog Who Walked Through Fire." *Reader's Digest*. April 1982.

Miscellaneous

Winner's Press Releases, Ken-L Ration Dog Hero of the Year—1992 Program, c/o McDowell and Piasecki, Chicago, Illinois.

TOR CLASSICS

☐	50424-0	ADVENTURES OF SHERLOCK HOLMES *Arthur Conan Doyle*	$2.50 Canada $3.25
☐	50422-4	ADVENTURES OF HUCK FINN *Mark Twain*	$2.50 Canada $3.25
☐	50420-8	ADVENTURES OF TOM SAWYER *Mark Twain*	$2.50 Canada $3.25
☐	50418-6	ALICE'S ADVENTURES IN WONDERLAND *Lewis Carroll*	$2.50 Canada $3.25
☐	50430-5	AROUND THE WORLD IN EIGHTY DAYS *Jules Verne*	$2.50 Canada $3.25
☐	50426-7	BILLY BUDD *Herman Melville*	$2.50 Canada $3.25
☐	50428-3	BLACK BEAUTY *Anna Sewell*	$2.50 Canada $3.25
☐	50432-1	CALL OF THE WILD *Jack London*	$2.50 Canada $3.25
☐	50438-0	CAPTAINS COURAGEOUS *Rudyard Kipling*	$2.50 Canada $3.25
☐	50434-8	A CHRISTMAS CAROL *Charles Dickens*	$2.50 Canada $3.25
☐	50436-4	A CONNECTICUT YANKEE IN KING ARTHUR'S COURT *Mark Twain*	$2.50 Canada $3.25

Buy them at your local bookstore or use this handy coupon:
Clip and mail this page with your order.

Publishers Book and Audio Mailing Service
P.O. Box 120159, Staten Island, NY 10312-0004

Please send me the book(s) I have checked above. I am enclosing $ _____
(Please add $1.25 for the first book, and $.25 for each additional book to cover postage and handling.
Send check or money order only—no CODs.)

Name _____
Address _____
City _____ State/Zip _____
Please allow six weeks for delivery. Prices subject to change without notice.

MORE TOR CLASSICS